CW01560598

Disorderly Lives

The Writer's Notebook

Short Story Collection No.1

Edited by Sandra Rose

Contents

Foreword

I had been toying with the idea of creating an online writers' group for a long time... Since 2010 to be precise, when I was studying for my English Literature degree and I would meet up regularly with my fellow students of my creative writing class to discuss our writing. But back then I was still studying part-time and working a full-time job, so I just didn't have the time to sit down and work out the details.

Then in November 2014, the idea returned to me.

The main feature of my writer's group had to be a free to enter short story competition. I was so fed up with looking up competitions only to find that they had an entry fee. At the time I didn't have spare cash lying around which I could use to enter those competitions, and I was certain that I wasn't the only writer who felt that way.

But, how was I to procure a prize for the winners of my competition without previously generating any revenue? Sponsorship from an established publisher was one of my first ideas, but it seemed a little old-fashioned in our social-media driven world.

That's when I had one of those eureka moments where you sit down for a ten minute tea-break on a snowy afternoon, and by the end of your cuppa you have a fully formed concept which you have to start work on immediately. I would independently publish a collection of winning stories and split the proceeds equally among the winning authors and myself... and so The Writer's Notebook came to life.

The website went live in December 2014, with the first contest launching on the 1st January 2015. Each month I set a new theme, and writers from all around the world can enter up to two stories per theme for free. I select three stories which are published on the site for two weeks along with a poll for readers to vote for a winner.

The first month was a nail-biter as I waited to find out if anyone would enter, but I am delighted to say that the competition took off immediately, and has gained popularity throughout its first year.

This book is the first collection of winning stories, at the beginning of each story you will see the monthly set-theme each story was entered into, and at the end of the book you will find some information about some of the authors. There is also a bonus story, written by myself.

Our winning authors have been incredibly supportive of my *writers doing it for themselves* concept, and have shown incredible patience as I gathered the winning stories throughout the year. Without them, and others like them who have shown faith in the competition, this collection would not have happened.

I hope you enjoy the stories, and if you would like to enter one of our competitions yourself you can find all the details on our website:
http://thewritersnotebookgroup.blogspot.co.uk/

You can also follow us on Facebook
https://www.facebook.com/writersnotebookcompetition

And on Twitter: @writers_sandra

January - Revenge

The Delivery

By Andrew Newall

Marcus Daniels had instructions to see Lennie, and was strongly advised to be prompt. He parked his car carefully on the grounds of his employer's estate where he was greeted by Lennie's secretary, formally dressed down to her thighs, who led him to Lennie's office. Crime lord Lennie Frame had his hands in every dirty business deal going down. Marcus had moved into a dangerous world working for him. As Lennie's newest recruit, he ran errands, keen to please, but perhaps too keen. On his first assignment, he grew overconfident on a simple delivery job, causing the cops to jump on Lennie's back. Marcus suspected Lennie had a few friends on the force, maybe even on the payroll, because the heat died down fairly quickly, but the word had been passed that the boss was unhappy with his new employee. Others had disappeared for less.

Lennie rose from his seat, the leather upholstery un-squashing its way back into shape.

9

'Marcus' he said, barely audible.

'Hello Mr. Frame'

A bead of sweat trickled down Marcus's neck, tickling, making him nonchalantly scratch the itch, trying not to show his fear while his heart pounded. Lennie was wide, rugged and softly spoken; a loose cannon hiding under the surface of a seemingly gentle demeanour.

'Let's get something straight, son. I don't like the law breathing down my neck' said Lennie quietly, but with menacing undertones. 'But I like you, Daniels. I like your style, I told you that before. So I'm going to give you another chance.' He handed Marcus a briefcase and a piece of paper.

'Deliver the case to the address on the note. The place is two hours away. You're taking it from A to B. That's it. No stops, no detours. Stick to the speed limit and you won't get pulled over like the last time. Can you handle it?'

'Absolutely Sir, and thank you very much.'

Lennie extended his hand and smiled. Marcus eagerly took it and felt his slight twenty-eight-year-old build hauled by the massive grip into a bear hug, ribs straining under the pressure.

'And don't fuck up this time' Lennie whispered into his ear. 'This one means a lot to me. I'll call you in a bit to see how things are going'. He gave Marcus a firm pat on the back.

'Oh and one more thing, Daniels' Lennie said as Marcus reached the door. 'Don't open the case.'

He gave Lennie a nod of assurance and left the room. Marcus was scared of Lennie but wanted his trust and was lucky to be getting this second opportunity. In fact, he knew he was probably lucky to be alive.

Outside, Marcus breathed a sigh of relief when he reached his car. The air had never tasted so good. He placed the case in the passenger seat and set off.

An act of chivalry had brought Marcus and Lennie together only a few weeks earlier, when Marcus visited a nightclub which Lennie owned. An overcrowded club, nobody stood a chance of escape in the event of a fire. The draft beer tasted like washing-up liquid. Scanning the clientele, he'd been distracted by a woman storming out of an office at the side, where a few customers sat. People standing around him blocked his vision but he saw a man catch up with her, spinning her around to face him. He barked something at her which Marcus didn't hear, though he could see it caused her some distress. The man threateningly ordered the customers sitting nearby to move. Marcus ambled his way through gaps and quickened his pace when the man grabbed the back of the woman's curled hair and gritted his teeth. In seconds, Marcus had reached him and had him floored; a foot slammed into his solar plexus ensured he'd stay where he was for the moment.

A second man saw the ruckus and threw himself at Marcus, only to be spun around and slammed into a table, previously occupied by the people who moved. He caught sight of the big man standing in the doorway, who introduced himself as Lennie Frame and calmly announced that Marcus had just effortlessly taken out two of his best men, a feat never achieved. He asked Marcus his name, where he worked. A factory? Lennie had other plans. He told Marcus he liked his style and could make a lot of money working for him if he was up for the job. He gave Marcus his phone number and didn't have to wait long for a call.

The events of that night played like a movie in his mind as he raced along the quiet country road. An hour into the journey, Marcus was making good time so he relaxed, waiting for Lennie to call, glancing occasionally at the briefcase on the passenger seat. Overconfidence crept in again. It was in his nature. He wanted to look in the case. He could pull over at the next lay-by and look in. There was one up ahead. He could pull in and have a quick look just to see what he was dealing with. No one would know.

As he approached the lay-by, one car already occupied the space. The car's hazards flashed and the bonnet was up. Any other day, he'd stop to offer assistance but not today, besides there would be another lay-by further on. However when the driver of the broken down car appeared from behind the bonnet with a shotgun and stood in the middle of the road, aiming it directly at him, he hit the brakes and the car screeched to a halt.

'Get out of the fucking car!' The man was desperate. He shook his gun.

'Please, I'm in a hurry. It's an emergency!' Marcus did his best to appeal to the gunman.

'One more time. I'm going to tell you one more time!'

One hand held the barrel of the gun tight. The other twitched on the butt, adjusting its grip. Marcus could tell the gunman didn't want to pull the trigger, but he couldn't risk pissing him off in case it went off by accident. The gunman moved towards him.

'GET OUT!'

'Okay. I'm coming. I just need to get something first' and he turned to get the case.

'Leave it! Leave it! Just get out now!' the man yelled and ordered Marcus to move away from the car.

He was too far away to try and tackle. The shotgun stayed locked on him while the carjacker got in the driver's seat. All the while, Marcus couldn't believe his bad luck.

'Please. I need that briefcase. I'm begging you. I'll be in deep shit if I don't get it.'

His words drowned in a screaming of tyres as he watched his own car speed off, the sudden sound of his mobile ringing sending a shiver through him. He answered, not taking his eyes off the car.

'It's me. Where are you?' Lennie was calm.

'Mr Frame, I'm about an hour away, sir.'

'Good.'

'Mr Frame there's something I need to tell you.' Marcus's voice started to quiver, picturing the man with the gun driving off, the briefcase in the passenger seat.

'It can wait. I need you to do me a favour' continued Lennie. 'I need you to pull over and open the case.'

'Open the case?'

Marcus watched the car driving into the distance, his situation worsening by the second. It was a long road and the car would tease him until it disappeared from view, and now Lennie wanted him to open the case? In his mind, he saw the carjacker looking down at the briefcase beside him, curious.

'Sir, something… something's happened.'

'What's happened? Have you opened it?'

'No, I haven't.'

'Well what's the problem? Open it now.'

The car was nearly out of sight. Marcus pictured the driver fiddling about with the locks on the briefcase, keeping one eye on the road at the same time as he flicks up the clips and opens the case…

A distant bang and the car exploded, flames shooting in all directions. Marcus stared at the flaming wreck of his vehicle, pieces of metal landing on the asphalt after being blasted into the air. A hit of shock, relief and anger overwhelmed him.

Yes, Marcus suspected Lennie had a few friends on the force, maybe even on the payroll. He now had no doubts that it was one of these friends who tipped Lennie off about an undercover cop posing as an eager new recruit in order to expose illegal operations.

He turned off his phone. A new plan was needed to bring down the powerful crime lord, so it was back to square one. It would be harder now. Marcus had run out of people to trust. He'd have to go it alone. But there was one possible advantage. Everybody now thought Marcus Daniels was dead.

The End

February – Bad Romance

My Lady
By Misty Mikes

'Would you do anything for me?'

Princess Montgomery stood in front of a full-length mirror, loosening her long, midnight hair from the heavy plait in which it was usually confined. Her reflected gaze met his, and his heart skipped a beat.

In that moment, he was struck by how beautiful she was. The mirror allowed him to admire her from front and back at once, and it took his breath away. The way her gleaming hair tucked over the graceful curve of her shoulder. The perfect curve of her waist, hugged lovingly by the red velvet dress before it flared elegantly into a full skirt.

Her face was even more beautiful. Her large blue eyes and full ruby lips had haunted many a sleepless night.

'Of course, my lady. I would do anything for you,' he answered eagerly. 'I would go to the ends of the earth. I would climb the highest mountain. I would swim to the bottom of the ocean if you but willed it. Anything.'

Those beautiful lips parted into a coy, pleased smile, and she turned to face him. 'I'm so glad to hear you say that. I want to be with you, my love. More than you could possibly know. There is only one small thing keeping us apart. Something I hope you can help me with.'

Her words were like music to his ears. Like sweet rain after a long drought, or the first hint of green after a long, hard winter. 'Anything, M'lady,' he cooed, unable to tear his gaze away from her guileless eyes.

Her skirts whispered gently against the rushes covering the floor as she stepped toward him. When she lifted one dainty hand to cup his cheek, he thought his heart might burst with joy. Her tiny palm was so soft; it felt as though she possessed rose petals in place of skin.

'It's my father, dearest one,' she murmured, her lips forming an adorable pout. 'He doesn't want us to be together.'

'The king?' he questioned. 'What does he have against me?'

'He's a silly old thing.' Her fingers caressed his cheek, making it difficult to concentrate. 'He wants me to marry some stuffy king. He wants to send me away to another country, where I will be all alone. It's terribly far away.'

As the sense of the words slowly sunk in, he felt a powerful rage building into an almost intolerable pressure in his chest.

'No!' he barked, and reached to take her small hand in his, holding it gently between his larger, rougher fingers.

'Yes,' she sighed, unhappily. 'So long as the king lives, we can never be together.'

He didn't even need to consider the implication of her words to know what needed to be done. 'Then the king will not survive the night,' he announced.

Her smile was like the dawn, growing slowly and warming everything it touched. 'Be careful, dearest. My brave one, be *terribly* careful.'

And then, oh then... She kissed him. He felt alive for the first time, as though he had hardly breathed before her kiss.

From that moment, everything was a blur. Dark hallways traversed stealthily, candlelight and a snoring figure still abed after a long night spent feasting, a splash of blood, yelling, angry faces, tapestry-covered walls blending together in a frightening kaleidoscope, but none of it mattered because she was his!

The deed was done, and he found himself back where he began, rushing to Lady Montgomery's room on silent feet.

The door to her bedroom sounded abnormally loud as he closed it behind him, the wood landing heavily against the stone wall. She was waiting for him there, sitting at her vanity combing the long, dark tresses he so admired.

When he entered, she dropped the comb onto her tray and turned without standing, her eyes alight with eagerness. 'Well?' she demanded. 'Is it done?'

His heart sang and he felt as though he was floating as he traversed the room so that he could gather her into his arms, laughter spilling from his lips. 'It's done! Now we can be together, forever!'

He pressed his lips to hers, and the world seemed to spin, twirling out of control. He didn't care. He held her in his arms, and that was all that mattered.

That is, until he didn't. Somehow, between one moment and the next, she had spun away from him. The room with all the trappings befitting a princess was gone, replaced with a blackness that seemed endless.

'M'lady?' he called. 'Where have you gone?'

Behind him, a familiar musical laugh caused him to twirl. There, floating in space, was Lady Montgomery's vanity mirror, with the Lady herself framed within.

'Thank you, my love,' she murmured, and pressed her lips to the glass.

Frightened, he leaped for the mirror, banging the glass with his fists as though the barrier might somehow break and release him, but it refused to yield even to his strong hands.

'M'lady! Help me!' he begged, but to his growing horror, she merely winked and disappeared from view.

A moment later, she reappeared holding a poker from the fireplace.

'M'lady? What are you...' Before he could finish the thought, she swung the heavy metal rod.

The glass shattered and he screamed, but there was no one to hear him.

The End

March – The Smoking Gun

Justice

By Ann Case

Swift feet pounded on pavement. The blue, then red, then blue, and blinding, bright white, lights flashed, closer with each bound. Behind her, she left a gaping hole, her car door hung open, slightly crooked on rusty hinges. Cell phone, almost too deep in her pocket. She got it, slippery in her sweaty hand. Frantic fingers mashed at buttons to flip on the video recorder. Something felt electric. Her eyes darted from the uneven terrain beneath her feet to the teeny tiny screen that seemed an ocean away in her hand. *What were they doing with him? He was already dead.* The savage nature of the attack, just down the street, just before she followed them. *What was that? retaliation? From the police? Kenny was a good kid.*

Rushing to the curb, it was a beachside park, the scene was circled in uniforms and people shouting, The gathering crowd pushed back away from the unfolding drama. She saw Kenny, his body lurching forward.

Then a gunshot, just one, suffocating the air from all other noise. The burst of noise cancelled the shouts, screams and bellows of emotional pain around the chaotic scene.

'No, no!' Was that her voice? 'What is this!?' Charlotte looked down at her brother. His large, strong body splayed in an unnatural position on the cold ground, desperation locked in his dead eyes.

Her knees buckled, the smell of iron filled her nose. Blood, deep and dark, pooled around her downed brother while MT's attended to hurt officers.

'What the fuck? Somebody help him!'

An MT looked over at her. An officer, on the perimeter, like a dog hearing a high pitch squeal nodded. MTs, Three of them, each with the snakes slithering up winged staffs adorning their uniforms, embroidered, permanent, descended on the body. They pronounced him dead. Lowering his lids, they summoned a stretcher.

'We'll need to wait for the coroner.' She heard one of them say.

There were arms around her, carrying her away. She fought, pummelling the arms and chests of the unknown people dragging her from the scene. Her flip flops scraped the pavement, then came off her feet. She was shoved into a car. The door slammed shut. It was her father, there, with her. A tear streamed down his anguished face. They hugged sobbing into each other's shoulders.

*

Outcries of anger burst from the frustrated people of the neighbourhood. Riots, and violence, fighting in the streets, this dominated the news, all while mourning the loss of Kenny. This brutality will not stand. With our downed brothers and sisters from Los Angeles to Ferguson, this one will not pass. A grand jury was imminent. Justice wasn't just for whites.

Until that day. They wanted to question Charlotte. Clear the air.

'So what can you tell us about that evening young lady?' Pink-skinned, Irish man, big crusty alcoholic nose. He sat casually on the edge of the desk, on the same side as Charlotte and her father. The officer's hands were folded in front of him, a plastic grin. The three stiff men, standing in the corners of the small office made her more nervous. Ominous and full of angst, she was sure they would pounce with even the slightest provocation. And the recording device, video and audio, trained on her. This wasn't real. Her father patted her hand.

'Just tell them what you saw.'

'I, well, um I was going home, and when I got to the corner, of, which is it?' She looked out of the glassed room office. A young male, about her age, white, stood looking in, pretending not to.

The pink officer stood up and flipped a chart showing a diagram where her brother was gunned down, complete with a satellite map of the area.

'Corner of Franklin and Third.' He tried to sound friendly, but ended up sounding tired and beat.

'Yes, that would be my usual way home, but I was coming from a friend's that night, not work. I drove this way, corner of Oak and fifth.'

'Ok, if you're sure. So what happened?'

After all was said and done, they crafted a story from the video they confiscated from her phone. Her words of no consequence. Of course, they had asked nicely, only the pink man's skin turned a deeper shade, almost crimson. He held his hand out, blue, watery eyes, bulging. Sighs, almost audible, shared by every person in the room as they viewed the broken, gut-wrenching scene play out on the miniature screen. Every person but Charlotte and her father. In the video, Kenny clearly had a gun and was coming towards Officer Banks. But Kenny didn't own a gun!

They were shuffled out. She saw Officer Banks, the murderer, with the young boy who was watching. She heard him call the officer dad.

*

At home, too quiet, her brother and his friends always filled the space. The friends didn't come anymore.

'Dad.' Charlotte rounded the corner into the kitchen.

'Yes.' Newspaper crinkling being set aside.

'This isn't right.'

'No. It isn't.'

'What do we do?'

Her father folded up the paper, stuffed it in the cubby next to his desk.

'Nothing.'

'They beat him papa. I don't know why. But they did.'

'If they say it happened that way, that's the way it happened. Can't do nothing about it.' More crinkling her father disappeared behind the news.

Charlotte couldn't stop feeling bad. Tears, a lot of them, fell in grief, then in anger, and at the end in deep frustration.

They buried her brother that day. Charlotte was leaving the grave site, the last one, lingering, murmuring final goodbyes. A figure approached. Her swollen eyes and cloudy mind had her confused.

He passed, and pressed a small metal stick in her hand. Hanging on, he pulled her close.

'This is what you do.'

He released her, and was gone. By the time the strangeness of the encounter settled and she turned to see who had approached her, the figure was gone. All she knew was he was white and male.

*

Late at night, the house was still. She crept across her bedroom with careful steps to avoid the creaks in the floor. A light switch snapped, her desk light illuminated a cone of light in the corner. She fumbled through her jacket pockets, and dug out the metal stick, a USB. She shoved it into the laptop port, double clicked the file. Chills went through her spine. The contents of the video file made the night long with uncertainty.

'Ready for school? You can stay home again if you need to.' Charlotte's father was pouring his morning coffee from the percolator on the stove while the Mr. Coffee in the corner stood idle.

'I'll go today.' Her eyes darted. *Should she tell him?*

'I gotta get an early start honey. See you tonight.' The lid snapped on his travel coffee mug. He grabbed his paper, slid it under his arm, and the door banged shut behind him.

Charlotte couldn't eat a bite. There would be no school today. She spent the night researching. Today she would go to the press.

*

Justice was served in the end. Officer Banks was brought up on charges, the others were being investigated. The headline, 'They killed Kenny! - New Video Evidence Exonerates.'

Weeks later the press was still around wanting to hear from the brave black girl that brought down the police department. Charlotte exited a large downtown building from an interview.

'Funny how things work out.' A voice behind her, she turned. He was white and male.

'Aren't you that cop's kid?' The white, male at the department when she was questioned, 'Officer Banks' son?'

'Guilty.'

She knew. It was him at her brother's gravesite. He was the purveyor of the final smoking gun.

'Why?'

'You think he was just violent on the job? You saved me too.'

'Thank you.' They stood close, their breaths steaming, intermingling, in the cool morning air.

'No, thank you.' The white male turned on his heel and headed down the street.

The End

April – Feeling a Fool

Rue the Day

By Katherine Hackett

Waking up was usually quite disorienting for Izzy Jones. She tended to either wake with her face shoved into the pillow, her mouth full of cotton, or with a jolt of sudden awareness. Occasionally, she had been known to fall out of bed with a panicked squeal.

Today was different.

Today, Izzy awoke with a clear thought in mind:

If Johnny Caulfield made so much as a *knock-knock* joke, she was going to murder him.

Quite simply, jail time would be worth it. It was entirely possible no court would convict her anyway. There were perhaps a half a dozen co-workers of theirs that would be willing to testify that she had been driven to it.

Yes, Izzy thought, wriggling into her tights and hopping on one foot, no one would blame her.

She approached the post with extreme caution later that morning, eyeing the wedge of envelopes hanging out of the letter box.

Last year she had received thirteen magazines, all subscribed to at exactly the right time to guarantee their arrival on this very day. The magazines had all been… questionable in nature. The one about the horses had been particularly disturbing.

And that was just the magazines! She had also received a few letters – one of which had an envelope filled with bright pink glitter, which had promptly coated her hands upon being opened. Johnny had not been able to conceal his glee at her sparkly hands. Another had contained a sonnet devoted to an extremely embarrassing incident at the last Christmas party. The words 'mistletoe' and 'Casey Jenkins' left buttock' had been included.

The last letter had been burned without reading.

Thankfully, a quick glance over the post told her that it was untainted by Johnny's maniacal machinations. The contents were actually quite dull. Izzy read them whilst munching on toast, trying to ignore the faintest sense of disappointment she felt at the sight of two bills and a letter from the Council.

Her car had also survived the morning.

One year it had been liberally coated with honey.

The resulting swarm of insects had sent her screaming back into her house.

Another year, she had only just sat down when she smelt the single most appalling scent to ever invade her nostrils. Again, she had fled the car without a backward glance, only determining the source of the smell much later.

A childish product aptly named 'Bottled Farts' was wedged under the driver's seat.

Mindful of these past incidents, Izzy got into the car with great caution, readying to flee at any second.

To her surprise, there was no unbearable odour or ominous buzzing of oncoming insects. In fact, the interior of her car looked exactly the same as it had the night before. Grey and clean.

Izzy hesitated, drumming her fingers on the steering wheel.

When nothing happened, she switched on the radio and waited.

The sound of country music filled the car, banjos and harmonicas twanging together.

Izzy turned the volume down and stared out of the window.

Could it be…?

Would this be the first April 1st she worked at the same office as Johnny Caulfield without a single prank?

Only time would tell.

The office was still standing when she arrived – not that she believed Johnny would burn it down or anything, smothering things in glitter or toilet paper was more his style. But still, there was *nothing*. Last year, he had posted Out of Order signs on every door of the building and covered the bathroom walls with pictures of past dictators.

And yet, today…

Nothing.

With a growing sense of unease, Izzy walked to her desk, responding to every greeting with only an absent smile or a nod. If her desk was bare of any sign of mischief, she wasn't sure what she would do. Rush Johnny to the hospital? Get down on her knees and thank God for this reprieve from the typically banal inanity of her least favourite day of the year?

When she saw the box on her desk, she actually breathed a hearty sigh of relief. She had never felt so comforted by the sight of what was probably a Jack-in-the-box or something rigged to explode in a shower of confetti.

She sat down at her chair (a jarring experience, marked by the lack of whoopee cushions) and gleefully snatched the box, ripping the wrapping paper off with reckless abandon.

It was…

A box of chocolates.

Izzy looked around, confused.

Where was Johnny, waiting for her reaction?

This was a bit tame, of course, but she'd take it. She opened the box, steeling herself for the sight of frogs or manure.

It was… they were actually chocolates. *What*?

Unwilling to risk actually tasting them, she broke one apart between her fingertips.

Caramel.

What?

This couldn't be right…

She shook the box violently, ignoring the stares of her fellow workers. Nothing.

Her cheeks felt a bit hot. Her foot was tapping restlessly, a nervous tic she thought she'd excised from her habits long ago.

What was going on?

She stood up abruptly, plonking the box back down on the desk. This was ridiculous. She would not let this stand.

She marched over to Johnny's desk, the dark scowl on her face enough to keep her co-workers at bay.

Johnny was bent over his desk, scribbling furiously. The little of his face that she could glimpse was creased in concentration. He was sticking out his tongue slightly as he worked. She told herself it was not cute in the slightest.

'Johnny!' She snapped.

He jolted upright out of his chair, still gripping his pen and paper. He gave her a slightly wild look, his eyes bloodshot.

'Izzy!' he exclaimed, backing up slightly.

'Chocolates?' She demanded, '*Chocolates*? That's the best you can do? Two years ago you convinced our boss to tell me it was Wear Your Pyjamas to Work Day! I showed up in my nightie, Johnny! My *nightie!* Have you lost your mind?!'

He eyed her warily, holding the piece of paper like a shield, 'Um, no… Have you?'

'I know you must be up to something! What is it? Hair dye in my shampoo? Ants in my lunch?'

'What? No, that's way too obvious!' Johnny protested, looking offended by the mere suggestion, 'I would *never* use ants. Anyway... did you not like the chocolates, then?'

'Like them?' Izzy paused, unsure of where he was going with this. She wasn't supposed to *like* his pranks, was she? 'Of course not. I can't even tell what they're supposed to do. Are they going to explode? Like the Christmas turkey of '09?'

Johnny stared at her, a look of dawning comprehension on his face, 'You thought it was a prank?'

'Obviously!' She rolled her eyes, 'your worst one yet, by the way.'

Johnny burst into sudden, slightly hysterical laughter, his cheeks flushed red. 'Oh God... it's April Fool's Day, isn't it?'

'Don't try that nonsense. Like I don't know you count the days until it arrives. I bet it's circled twice on your calendar with little hearts all around it.'

'I forgot... I was so focused on *this*,' He gestured with the paper in his hand, 'that I actually forgot! I guess you can have it now anyway, I've been going over it for days and I'm sick of the sight of it.'

Izzy took the proffered sheet of paper and examined it with a look of intense scrutiny, convinced that this must be it; the Ultimate Prank Johnny had been leading up to.

It was another sonnet.

It involved the words 'love' and 'you.'

Izzy stared at it until the words blurred.

The realisation dawned on her slowly.

Her first thought was this:

Johnny was going to tell *so many* knock-knock jokes at their wedding.

Surprisingly, her next thought did not involve the desire to murder him.

The End

May – Obsession

Blush

By Brian Cofflin

My shin looks like a half-finished chicken dinner; an undercooked one given the fresh, red blood that streaks across the bone. If you can see the snowy white surface of your tibia, you're in trouble. I know that, as well as I know every inch of this Accident and Emergency department. This new wound sits alongside older ones and together they map out a sorry story on my skin. Scars instead of sentences tell the ugly truth of my life.

Nurse Ryan floats in. Mid-twenties. Graceful mover. Always gorgeous. I'm breathless just watching her.

'There she is: the swab in a bob.'

She blushes and I see the shy smile that flicks a million light switches within me.

'What have you done to yourself this time?' she asks, peering down.

The smile soon levels out.

'Good lord,' she says. 'What *have* you done?'

Her expression screams concern.

'Flipped her at sixty on a sharp one near Crabtree Farm. Rolled five times apparently. Stopped three feet from a sheer drop and a half-mile roll to the next county. Finished with the pedal imbedded in my leg.'

'What did you do?'

'I rolled free from the wreck. Pulled it out with my bare hands.'

She looks at me like I'm crazy and maybe I am.

'You are joking?' she asks.

I shake my head.

'Life of a rally driver Nurse Ryan. Could have been worse. Missed a group of spectators by an inch. Could've killed them. That would have really hurt. No one would miss me. But the spectators? They're all aunts and uncles, parents, children……'

Tina Ryan sets about her work. Within minutes she has corralled the requisite paperwork, led me to a private cubicle, cleaned out a gash as big as a crater and booked an emergency consultancy. The result is a surgical appointment. She stays with me while I wait. Holds my hand. Watches me go to Theatre. All the while, she wears that look. Forget concern, she looks like she cares.

Two days later and I'm right as rain. I use my crutch to hail a cab and bore my driver with the same small talk he probably despises. Thing is, I don't know what else to say. Not sure how to be interesting. I settle for the baseline mediocrity I've achieved my whole life. 'Busy today mate? What time you on until? What time did you start at?'

He leaves me near the Bridge, a half-mile from home. Takes a while to walk the last bit. Doesn't matter. Last lap is always the longest. Happy for it too. It'll make me tired. I find sleep hard to come by sometimes. To do with temperature I think. My bed is cold sometimes.

I swallow a pill and put head to pillow. I think about how pretty Nurse Tina Ryan looked earlier. Think about that time she spent with me, caring. I remember how soft her hands felt, even under the cold, sterile barrier of surgical gloves. The hair bob, like a modern day Cleopatra, the smooth skin on flushed cheeks. And still no wedding ring. I wonder why that is.

I let the pain killers and the airy feeling of being in love lead me into peaceful sleep.

*

I stagger from the garage to my front door, stop to get a breath and re-start. I make it four yards, just into the hall before I fall on one knee. Manage to lift the handset. This time it's bad. So bad I won't be able to start a car, never mind drive one. Left hand is twice as big as normal in places, thin and flat in others. More ironies to be found. Hardness and mush. Blue and red. Bone and skin. Emergency operator listens to a whole lot of gibberish as I gave her the distorted tale of events that my agonised mind composes.

I succumb to the pain and it all goes black. I waken again to find a paramedic attacking my door with an axe.

Climbs inside. Checks me for vitals. Then I'm on the stretcher, in an ambulance. Hospital ahead.

I wake intermittently, in a feverish hybrid of knowing and pretending and hoping and wondering. A raft of skewed thoughts rush through my mind like taunting charlatans with made up faces. I look all around and take nothing in. Feel a hand I cannot see. Hear a voice I cannot fathom.

Enough. Snap out of it. Have to focus. Blink and you'll pass out. Pass out and you'll miss her. How does hospital admission work when you turn up in an ambulance? Do you even go to A & E? Or do you go to Theatre? Go straight to jail, do not pass go, do not collect 300. Or was it 200? Where am I again?

Ah, see something I know. Rectangular lights, ones with the dimples and the bulbs you can look at without them burning holes where your eyes used to be. Hear a ripping noise, tilt my head. See a little plastic hose. Good, drugs are coming. Was starting to feel a little sick. Right hand feels good, left feels like I'm shaking hands with the devil. Where are those drugs? And the lights, where did they go? Why am I in an elevator?

And where is Tina Ryan.

Suddenly I'm parked, and my throat feels like a battleground as fancy aftershave fights with disinfectant. I open my eyes and find a man in a suit. Nice tie, nicer shirt. Can't really move now. Can't even talk. Feel woozy, lighter than air. The man in the suit looks like he's concentrating; like a snooker player you see on telly, in behind the black and hunting for a red to hit. Mr Nice Suit isn't alone. Others are with him, their words coming out in one long drone like a vinyl on slow play. They are pointing at something and touching it too. Don't know what it is. Not my hand anyway. At least, I don't think it's my hand.

Soon I am off again. This time I'm able to lift my head slightly. Seem to be wearing blue paper. Some chap asks me to count to ten. Easy. I can do that in my sleep. Get to four. What comes after four? Oh yeah, five, then six, then…

I wake up. I see Mr Nice Suit and his smile is tender but in no way arousing. Where the hell did Tina Ryan go? Haven't seen her at all during this visit.

I awake for a second time. Everything is clear now. My mind is no longer drunk with pain and dope. I am able to appraise. I look down and find a tightly wrapped stump where my left hand used to be. It's the size of a basketball and tied so tight to the bed rail that I cannot move it an inch. My vision picks out the form of a pretty lady. She's sitting by my bed. She's half-smiling, half-crying, looking relieved and pensive in one beautiful face.

'Well?' she asks, sniffling.

I smile. Always got a smile for Nurse Ryan.

We share a long silence. I'm no great people-reader and even if I was, there isn't too much a sixty-two year old man could read from a pretty snip in her mid-twenties. She thinks I'm a rally driver. I wonder if now's the time to address this.

'Thirteen times in the last year,' she says, holding her hanky like a shield against her face.

Counting to ten was hard enough when I got anaesthetised. Why is she talking about thirteen?

'Thirteen times you've been to A & E in the last year.'

'Is it really that many?' I ask.

I know the answer.

'The police looked in your garage.'

"So what?" I want to say, but I could never be rude to her.

'They say…… that you inflicted the wound yourself. And not just once either. You hit yourself up to *four* times…… with a *mallet*.'

"Of course!" I want to say, "I'm a man's man working with primitive tools on my machine." Good, strong men do that. Accidents happen. But I see something in her face. Comprehension.

'And all your other injuries,' she says. 'You did them *all* to yourself. Didn't you? *Deliberately*.'

I'll come up with a retort, a quip, something smart to wrestle back control of this spiralling situation. It's how I am, a man for all seasons, made of sturdy stuff. Happy-go-lucky. Type of guy who could find a ring for that naked wedding finger. Give her manly, give her hero, give her honesty.

'I'm lonely,' I say.

Feels like a spirit possessed my tongue. That wasn't me. I didn't mean that. Quick, say something else. For God's sake man, rectify this, or you'll never forgive yourself. Come up with something good, come up with it now.

'I love you,' I say.

Her cheeks blush. She turns quickly. She runs off, weeping.

The End

June – In the Blink of an Eye

Foretoken

By SM Cadman

"In Einstein's equation, time is a river. It speeds up, meanders, and slows down. The new wrinkle is that it can have whirlpools and fork into two rivers. So, if the river of time can be bent into a pretzel, create whirlpools and fork into two rivers, then time travel cannot be ruled out."

Michio Kaku

I miss Connor, I thought about our days jumping the railroad tracks, dodging trains, talking about our first high school physics class together. He was more concerned with it being able to help him throw a football further than knowing the physical space we inhabited was actually part of something much greater.

At fourteen, we were a mismatched duo. He was obsessed with becoming the next rising football star on the Freshman Knight's team at Scranton Pennsylvania High and I was a geek into science and mathematics, but somehow we vibrated on exactly the same string.

I knew he wasn't athletic enough to make it onto the team but I supported his dream. He was bullied by our peers and I often defended his callous behaviour as being misunderstood. But sometimes it scared me just how far he would push the limits of normal human boundaries and how cruel he could be.

'Jump you idiot!' Connor yelled out to me.

'You're the fast quarterback, not me!' I said. He shook his head in disbelief, 'Here, like this!' he jumped across the railroad tie while looking back at me but mistook his footing and fell to the ground hitting his head on the steel beam of the track.

'Oh my god!' I ran over to check on him, 'Damn! That was fun. But I slipped on something...' he said while laughing lying across the tracks, he reached down to his shoe with his right hand, 'There I feel it, something metal is stuck to the bottom my shoe, what is it?' he asked. Worried, I moved down to look at his shoe, I peeled off a flattened penny from his sole, it had a strange circle with a stretched figure eight enclosed within it.

'Jesus, who cares, it's a flattened penny, we have to get you off the tracks, a train might come!' I said pleading with him.

'It's weird. I can hear what you're saying but somehow I can't see you anymore,' I saw a river of blood flowing out from the back of his head while he lay upon the steel beam.

'Connor? CONNOR! Stay with me!' I yelled out, 'It doesn't work like that, keep the penny close to you. It will remind you of things that shouldn't be, a token from the future,' he shut his eyes and died.

***

'Adam, wake-up! You're going to be late getting to that meeting at DARPA, your Heisenberg blimp-thingy,' Natasha my administrative assistant said in her Russian accent while trying to wake me. I had just put my head down to rest for a moment and I was out like a light.

'I think you're confusing Hindenburg with Heisenberg,' I laughed and sat up, 'The Heisenberg Uncertainty Principle has nothing to do with Zeppelin's or blimps,' I responded while cracking a smile.

'Gavno! Really? Anyways you better get moving,' she said.

'Did you just swear at me in Russian?' I asked, 'Maybe...' she said while sticking her tongue out at me. I smiled and collected my papers and laptop and headed out. She was adorable when she was saucy with me.

She caught me at the exit, 'Wait! You forgot your lucky penny,' she said as she folded it into my hand, I smiled and left the building.

***

'A particle given enough energy can travel back in time so that a particle field creates a temporal rift, it's a side effect of the light bending experiment,' I paused for a moment anticipating their reactions, 'We can travel in time,' I explained.

'Adam, have you tested this yet?' Edward asked, 'Yes,' I replied. 'With great success, I was able to view something from an alternate perspective and jump back to a moment in my own past...' I said.

***

'Jump you idiot!' Connor yelled out to me.

'You're the fast quarterback, not me!' I said.

I arrived exactly the moment before his death and grabbed the flattened penny from the tracks. I stood in the bushes and watched Connor jump the tracks and land firmly upright. I smiled and looked down at the penny in my hand as I readjusted the quantum LED transponder. I reprogrammed it to my present, sent the particle beam out and jumped forward back into time.

As I walked through the light, Natasha's voice called out to me, *You're back!* Surprised, I rubbed my eyes as a beam of light flashed off my hand and bounced up into my eyes. I blinked. There was a wedding band on my left ring finger. I felt a warm kiss across my lips and I collapsed.

'Just breathe. This always happens when you return,' she was holding my hand while smiling, 'Connor called, he's in jail again,' she winced as I shut my eyes trying to comprehend what was happening.

'He's done it again... hacked another database. They picked him up. As usual, he was yelling about the future and things not really meant to be,' Natasha went quiet.

'Not meant to be?' I asked as I dozed off, 'Don't worry, I'll post bail for him. He'll probably insult me for doing so but he's your best friend, even if he's a total abusive, narcissistic fuck up,' she said.

***

Natasha and Connor arrived home later that evening. After my jump back, I spent the afternoon trying to acquaint myself with my new life. My best friend was still alive and I now had a wife, I looked at wedding photos and Googled information about myself and others playing catch up to this new world order.

When I pulled up information on Connor, I was dumbfounded at what I encountered. He was expelled from high school at sixteen for hacking through the school board's records database attempting to change SAT scores for other students. At seventeen, in another article I read he was expelled from a second alternative school for cyber-stalking and bullying. At twenty, he was charged with drug possession with intent to sell Heroin; at twenty-five he was in jail after an attempted assault of a young woman and then he was also implicated in the disappearances of several other people who had gone missing around the same time also. It went on and on, news article after news article from hacking to missing people, his life had been a disaster. I kept thinking to myself, *what the fuck have I done?*

Connor busted into the library where I had been reading at my computer, there was blood all over him, 'It's not supposed to be this way, you don't fucking get it,' Connor said to me, 'What do you mean?' I asked, 'You saved me, you weren't supposed to!' he said, 'I looked at

44

the data, I was supposed to save you and all those people!' I stood speechless, staring at his hands covered in red.

'She's fucking dead. I killed her,' he dropped to his knees and started sobbing, 'Now listen to me, go back,' he handed me the flattened penny with the figure eight enclosed within a circle.

'Take the penny, put it back on the tracks, in this life I was never meant to be now look what you've done! They're all dead!' he screamed. Frightened I stood there shaking, and began to cry then asked what I had been dreading, 'Where's Natasha?' he looked at me then pointed to her car in the driveway, I ran out to the car.

I didn't see her at first, she was lying down across the backseat, the back of her head bloodied, her breath was rattling, 'Natasha!' I called out to her, 'I'm here, after I bailed him out he took me to the tracks to show me like he had with the others, to prove his point. I slipped and fell as they did,' she handed me a flattened penny but this one was blank, 'It split into another perspective Connor said, you *must* return, I love you...' she closed her eyes and died.

This wasn't the Grandfather Paradox it was something much worse, 'Now go! Jump back and fix this shit!' Connor yelled. Crying I ran back into the house and found the Quantum LED transponder, I turned it on and jumped back. I placed the penny back on the tracks before I saw the two of us approaching then hopped into the bushes besides the tracks and prayed. I watched Connor die again.

The End

July – Isolation

The Space Child
By Meghashri Dalvi

He was famous even before he was born.

The frenzy had started when that idea was put forward first. It heightened when his parents agreed. It reached a big high when the conception was declared. And it reached its peak when he was born.

The Space Child, they called him. The first ever child to be conceived and born in space. The pioneer of the Final Frontier. The first one, and the only one.

Of course his mother was exhausted and tired at the end of it. And his father absolutely weary. But it did not matter. The experiment was successful.

Then the entire army of people had taken over. The special nurses, the nutritionists, the psychologists, the teachers, and the others.

His father visited the space station once in a while. His mother came more often. She watched in amusement, and cuddled him occasionally. It was not easy for her to do more in front of the omnipresent cameras.

He continued to grow. Unaware of his unusual circumstances. A healthy boy of excellent intelligence. He knew nothing beyond his cubicle in the space station. He played there, took his tumbles there, and learnt to walk there.

When he was one year old, his nurse took him to the next cubicle. As a special birthday treat. His parents cherished the day, the President blessed the occasion, and a handful of select journalists covered the event. The world celebrated one complete year of the special boy.

He was totally shocked to see so many new things. The balloons, the cake, and of course the people. Perhaps more shocked because of the realization that a place existed outside his room.

No one noticed that then, but it was a beginning. The beginning of a lonely boy's search for his self.

*

Then he was put on an extensive educational course. His teachers were the best on Earth, specially trained to take care of him. He was taught the alphabets, the words, and then the sentences. Later some science, some general knowledge, and some maths. His grasp was exceptional for everything he was taught. The scientists attributed it to his hunger for new things. But he alone knew that it was to battle his loneliness.

There was a slight uneasiness about the whole experiment after a few years. On Earth, a small group was voicing concern about this healthy bright boy. About his future and his life. About his growth and his normalcy. But the voice was small, mainly because the experiment was successful after all. He was the perfect space child, being groomed for a long life among the stars.

He slowly learnt about it all. About being different from the rest of the humankind. Even different from his space station crew. They were born and brought up on Earth. And they frequently took long breaks to visit their family on Earth. He was the only one who had never set foot on Earth.

He often found himself staring at the large blue globe in space. The swirling white clouds and the glistening oceans. He tried to imagine of life there. Children going to schools in colourful school buses, filled with their merry noises. Children playing and fighting and then getting cuddled by their parents. Parents telling stories and jokes, sharing laughs with the kids.

He wanted to experience all that. Even the occasional punishments. He very much wanted to taste the life on Earth.

One day he gathered enough courage to ask his mother. The poor woman braved to be very factual about it. She explained about the zero gravity of the space station and the heavy gravity of Earth. She described the crowded places and low hygiene there. She also elaborated about the pollution and various diseases.

In the end he still wanted it all.

Back on Earth his mother cried for days. Thinking about her little boy. She helplessly called her ex-husband, but he was not too serious. It is part of the package - he simply tried to justify.

She thought hard and then decided to join the group sympathizing with the Space Child.

*

He was eight, when for the first time he met other children. The young visitors from Earth wore heavy protective suits and glared at him from a distance. But he did not notice. He discovered that he could talk endlessly. Showing them, and playing the perfect host.

The euphoria lasted only for a short time. The children were back to Earth and he was lonely again. Now fully proficient in four languages, excellent in maths, expert in solving logic puzzles, skilled musician, and a top-class student of history. But still a very lonely boy.

He had accepted it though. He now knew that his future lay in space. He would be the first one to go trekking in space. Looking for new worlds and newer life-forms. He knew that his special spaceship was getting ready on Earth, and his journey was being planned meticulously.

He also knew that the time would come soon. Maybe a couple of years. He thought of the long life ahead. Life spent with machines, robots, and the dark emptiness of space. Life confined to the spaceship with a few exchanges with the earth-based crew. He longed for company, but accepted that he wouldn't have any. Ever.

He had heard about the relationships people had on Earth. About having cousins, neighbours, friends, and even enemies. About love, caring, and anger. About the tender love between man and woman. He wondered if he will ever experience that. He sometimes imagined being here with a partner. A beautiful girl with large lovely eyes and delicate body. He imagined her smiling at him and he caught himself smiling back.

Why? Why me? Why anyone for that matter? Why this experiment? Why go in space? Why leave the splendours of Earth? Why bother?

He knew that no one will answer him. The Earth people were very careful while talking to him. They treated him specially. Like Royalty. Like a fragile expensive object. Like someone whom they will never see among themselves. Like someone to be protected. Kept away from the disturbing answers.

So he continued to live the way they wanted. Protected, pampered, cajoled, and very much alone.

*

When he was twelve, the spaceship was ready. The celebrations on Earth were almost like the celebrations of his birth. Only this time he understood everything. Everything he meant to the Earth people. Their dreams, their faith, and their hopes.

He was fully trained to take over the ship. The technicalities and the formalities - his sharp mind had mastered them all.

The President came over to the space station with a few journalists. His mother had by now accepted his fate and came up, too. He smiled and shook hands with all of them. His eyes rested on his mother for an extra moment. But then he firmly moved on. He had no expectations from anyone now.

His brave shoulders were now eager to take on the mammoth task. Prepared to live alone and survive the confines of the space ship, he was ready for the long journey.

He left the space station for the first time. His only home till now. From the new spaceship he saw the space station all over. It looked so big and yet so cosy. He knew he would not be coming back to it. He could not help letting out a tiny sigh.

Inside the spaceship he took a hard look. This would be his home for the next so many years. For a fleeting moment he thought of the Earth homes he had seen in pictures. Then he brushed the thought aside. There was no need to long for what you do not have and what you will not have - he reasoned himself.

He took all checks. Satisfied, he raised his thumb to the Earth crew.

They fired.

The Space Child finally started towards the stars. Where he was supposed to belong. In the vast emptiness of space. Confident, anxious, curious, and all alone.

The End

August – Dystopia

The Bagman

By Vaun Murphrey

Like the Northern carpet bag vultures of old who descended on the South after the Civil War Era had ended, Bagmen had no code of honour. They swept into failing towns with their miracle tonics and fertilizers guaranteed to grow food out of the dead earth, burlap sacks on their backs and shark-like smiles in force.

Shy watched the hunchbacked silhouette of the Bagman grow larger at the crest of each hill on the narrow clay road. Today she was lookout for the northern barricade. Shy ran her fingertips down her blow tube, from where it rested against her collarbone all the way to her knee. Leaves flipped in the gentle breeze. The too short wet season had just ended, and the foliage of the forest was green and full – perfect cover in her tree stand.

The Bagman sped his pace when he saw the stacked log gate. He came into dart range and set his load by his feet then whistled the sign for those who wished to trade. His sun-browned face tilted this way and that.

Shy heard the creak of the rope ladder as it smacked into the bark of her tree. She hooked a toe in the loop handle of the trapdoor and lifted it just in time for Zeke's dark head to emerge.

Zeke peered over the railing as he fingered the string of his bow across his chest. His mouth went into a sideways frown, and he wiggled his nose as if it itched before he whispered, 'Run him off?'

Shy plucked a dart out of her waist pack. Zeke saw the colour of the feathered dart tail. Blue for sleep not red for death.

Zeke shook his head, 'You can't bring him inside without Elder Mike's approval, Shy. He won't give it. Momma wouldn't want you to risk banishment just to search for medicine. Are you a thief now?'

Another shrill whistle split the air. That decided it for Shy. Abe was sick, and Momma said in the old days there used to be medicine for just his kind of illness. The Bagman was a long shot, but she'd risk it. Abe's bright smile swam in her mind's eye as Shy leaped onto the rough-hewn rail then hopped to the narrow aerial trail of boards that connected the watcher's post to the barricade.

Zeke followed after an exasperated huff.

Shy put the smooth tube to her lips and blew with just the right amount of force. The Bagman cried out, stumbled forward two steps and then fell to the ground.

Zeke hissed in her ear, 'What if the brigands have us staked out, Shy? They could get all of us if we go down.'

She shrugged at her younger brother as she wrapped a rappelling rope around her forearm. Shy planted her bare feet on the outer edge of the barricade, 'I guess you'll have to cover me then, Zekey.'

Shy pushed off. Three quick, controlled falls and her calloused palms were warm from the pressure of her sliding grip on the rope. She crouched, listening to the forest for any sounds of interrupted birdsong or small animals running through the underbrush. Nothing yet.

Zeke clicked his tongue twice to let Shy know he had an arrow ready.

The Bagman's chest rose and fell in a pattern of deep relaxed sleep. This close Shy saw his clothes were rags. His feet were blistered and painful looking. A stranger in a strange land in bad shape. A pang of conscience struck her. She couldn't just leave him here even *if* he didn't have what they needed. It would be tantamount to death. The forest was a wild, untamed place beyond their tiny pocket of waning civilization, filled with hungry predators of the four-legged *and* two-legged variety.

Shy heard the crackle of the underbrush right before Zeke clicked the alarm. On the crest of the closest hill a huge animal burst from the tree line. As it reoriented, Shy got a good view of curled tusks and spiked fur.

Boar! Blast it. Their hide was too thick for one of her puny darts to penetrate. Zeke wouldn't have much luck with an arrow either. Shy needed a steel-tipped spear.

A furious snort and then the boar charged.

The Bagman sat upright, and Shy about jumped out of her skin. He rolled to his feet and pulled a crossbow from under his ragged cloak, sighted and squeezed the trigger. Front hooves folded under the running beast, and it furrowed the clay road until it came to rest with a bolt between the eyes.

Shy twirled her blow tube like a staff and knocked the Bagman behind the knees. He fell but retained his hold on the crossbow.

Zeke shouted, '*Oy!* Drop your weapon or I drop you!'

The Bagman grumbled, 'A fine way to greet a man who saved your life.'

Shy stayed ready, 'How are you not out? I scored on your neck Bagman.'

He pulled his cloak aside to reveal a leather collar with her dart still jutting from it. The Bagman's blue eyes sunk into dark hollows. He looked worn and trampled by his travels. 'I seek shelter with a gift of meat.'

The formal phrase made Shy straighten her shoulders. At least he had manners. He also didn't look as old up close as he had from the watcher's post. Maybe four or five years her senior she guessed. Young to be a solitary traveller. Shy snorted; Bagmen were tough buggers.

She snapped a finger over her head for Zeke to lower the scaling platform. The complicated pulley system was easier than trying to move the stacked logs without help.

'You'll have to assist with the carcass and then climb on your own.'

The Bagman fastened his crossbow to a belt around his waist, 'No, I ride up on my kill. You and the boy can pull it up.'

She cocked her chin, 'You hear that, Zeke?' Shy grew worried when her brother didn't answer. The hulking outline of Elder Mike blocked out the sun; her heart sunk.

Elder Mike boomed, 'This is your last transgression Shy. I hereby cast you from Glen!'

Zeke's voice shrieked from beyond, *'No!'*

Elder Mike turned his upper body to order Zeke's silence. Shy didn't take the time to think before she loaded a dart and took aim. The small red missile found its mark in Elder Mike's second chin. His limp body toppled forward and landed with the crunch of shattered bone.

Shy gave serious eyes to the Bagman, 'Get that boar to the wall. I'll be right back.'

The Bagman answered with a nod of respect.

When Shy cleared the top Zeke had an arrow notched and ready. Three of Elder Mike's lackey's had their hands high in surrender.

Zeke asked, 'What now Shy?'

Shy tossed the platform down and heard it bang on the log barrier.

'That's *Elder* Shy Zekey.' She pointed beyond to the clearing that held their town. Smoking cook fires blurred the skyline. Her next words were for their hostages, 'Go tell the rest I'm in charge now. No more favourites. All our supplies will be split equally between every family. Say anything other than that, and I find out, you're dead men.'

After they had run to spread the word, Shy helped Zeke pull the heavy load of man and beast to the top.

The Bagman touched his forelock before he leapt off then grabbed a rope to help.

When they finished, Shy wiped the sweat from her lips before it leaked into her mouth as she asked, 'What should I call you Bagman?'

He grunted and adjusted his burlap sack over his shoulder, 'Luke is fine. I'm not a Bagman.'

Shy demanded, 'What are you then?'

Luke produced a cloth badge from his leather jerkin. The symbol drawn in faded ink was an old one, one not seen in these parts for many, many years. Two snakeheads kissed with their tails wound around a staff.

Shy's heartbeat doubled in excitement. Whether fortune had smiled on her and her people remained to be seen. A healer could be a two-edged blade, a master of both life *and* death.

Zeke slung his bow across his body and offered Luke a hand to shake, 'Welcome to Glen Healer Luke.'

The End

September – Illusion

Tom, Tom the Baker's Son

By Nicola A. Ferguson

'Oh Anna I'm so worried about Tom,' Louise sat down at the kitchen table opposite her sister. She picked up her glass of wine and took a deep slug, ignoring its subtle raspberry and blackcurrant notes, with just a hint of cinnamon. Anna frowned; her sister was not one to get drunk during the day.

'He's been going out at night and staying out, not returning home for hours, sometimes not even until the next day. When he does come back he just ignores me, never mind the state he's in.'

'It's a just phase he's going through. All teenagers have them.' Smiling sympathetically Anna reached across the table and took her sisters hand in hers; rubbing her thumb lightly over Louise's skin, 'Sometimes you have to give them a little freedom.'

Both women looked round as door creaked open and Tom sauntered into the kitchen. Tall, with the long, lean build of an athlete, sunlight gleaming off his glossy black hair he looked the picture of health. "Tom. Come and say hello to your aunt Anna" Barely glancing at his mother or aunt, Tom didn't bother himself with a reply; instead he helped himself to some milk and simply left.

'Do you see what I mean? He didn't even acknowledge us. I just don't know what I'm going to do. Punishment doesn't work – it just makes him worse. I really am at my wits end.'

'What does David say about all this?'

'You know David; he likes to keep the peace. He's always indulging him, buying him this that and the other. Sometimes I feel the adoption was a big mistake. He's just too much for us. Maybe we should take him back.'

'Louise, don't say that. It'll get better really it will. This time next year his behaviour will have improved no end and you just won't recognise him.'

'Here's to better days then,' Louise raised her glass, reached across the table and toasted to the future with her sister. In the background against the musical 'ting' of the glasses they could hear Tom banging about upstairs, oblivious to the pain he was causing his mother.

*

Night had just fallen as Tom prepared to leave the house. Both his parents were finally asleep and although they had locked all the doors, pocketing the keys, the window of the upstairs bathroom had been left open. Climbing through the window without a sound, Tom jumped lightly down onto the flat roof of the garage. He could almost be a cat burglar. Perhaps his escape this evening would teach his parents to keep all of the windows closed in future. It was a good area but you never knew who was out on the prowl these days.

From the roof it was an easy descent into the garden, Tom's favourite part of the house.

It's not that Tom wasn't grateful to his parents for adopting him. He was, very much so. He didn't remember too much about the first years of his life, but he knew they were harsh and Tom understood that he could have languished in the adoption centre for many years, constantly growing older and more unattractive. Everyone wanted to adopt the little cute ones to cuddle and pass round, not a big boy like him with a mind of his own.

Tom headed off down the street at a brisk trot. A bus wasn't an option of course, and it would take him an hour or so to get into the centre of town. He was young and fit though, and he loved being out at night, relishing the darkness and the fresh breeze in his hair. There were some cute girls in the neighbourhood and maybe if anyone else was out and about this evening he wouldn't have to head all the way into town. Unfortunately most of the houses he passed were in darkness and the streets were silent and deserted. He would just have to head to Connolly's Bar; it was always full of life.

*

Tom made good time and once he reached Connolly's he stood on the opposite side of the road for a while, gazing at the lurid neon sign and the crowds of scantily dressed young people hanging around outside. So much life and vitality, it was a shame to let it go to waste. Tom's breathe quickened slightly and moving further down the road he found a suitable place to cross, dodging the traffic. He wasn't particularly distinguished looking and any CCTV was unlikely to highlight him as a potential threat, even if he had been standing, staring for a quite a while.

There was an alley that led to the back door of the club that would be perfect for his purposes this evening. Keeping to the deepest and darkest shadows, avoiding the weak pool of yellow light cast by the one solitary bulb illuminating the night, Tom slunk down the alley. The reek of stale urine, acrid and pungent stung his nose followed quickly by the stench of garbage and much worse. Tom gagged, a thin stream of bitter fluid flooding his mouth.

Inside Connolly's the hunt was in full swing, girls chasing boys, boys chasing girls and everything in-between. Tom knew that the club would soon regurgitate one of its inhabitants into the alley, which was a popular hangout for all sorts of nefarious activity. Then the real hunt would begin. Tom had spent many hours here as a voyeur, just sitting watching so he knew he was unlikely to be disturbed. Hunkering down onto his haunches, his emerald green eyes narrowing into slits, Tom welcomed this first quiet phase of the chase - he was a patient boy after all. Insensible to the passage of time, Tom waited and watched, staring at the moon as clouds scudded across its surface.

In his peripheral vision Tom sees sudden movement. The door opens, just a crack, then with a bang it slams against the side of the building, light flooding the alley. A man emerges accompanied by a little girl, no more than five or six years of age. Her long blonde hair is curled into ringlets, swinging down past her waist she is dressed in a blue and white pinafore, as if ready to attend school.

Even from a few meters away Tom can clearly detect the man's pulse, beating in his wrinkled neck, elevated in anticipation of the night's pleasures. Tom stands and stretches, loosening muscles that have stiffened in the long wait.

Stealthy he advances but there's almost no need, the man is so engrossed in his business he doesn't notice Tom's presence until it is much too late and Tom is already on top of him.

*

'Tom! Tom! Where have you been? Just look at the state of you. You're a bad, bad boy. You know it's not safe to be out on your own at night.' Rather sheepishly Tom allows his mummy to towel him dry, even permitting her to dab the congealed blood from his chin with not even a growl.

'Look, you're bleeding Tom. David, look Tom's bleeding.'

'Nonsense, he's just been out hunting again. Let him have his fun, he won't come to any harm.'

'I know darling, but I just worry about him so much. With all these murders going on, it's not safe for a person let alone a cat to be out at night.'

With a chirp of welcome Tom jumps up onto his daddy's knee, relishing the familiar smell of yeast and flour. Settling down he allows his fluffy black tummy to be stroked and enjoys the pull of his daddy's rough hands round his ears.

'Well I'm not standing for it. Look at the state of this towel. It's filthy and it's got all sorts on it. I know you don't like it but I'm taking him into the vet next week to be castrated. It'll stop his wandering if nothing else.'

Tom ponders that he doesn't particularly like his mummy very much. Daddy is a lot more relaxed, and really it would be far nicer with just the two of them. Warm, dry and with his appetite sated for now, Tom thinks maybe mummy won't come home from work tomorrow. Purring contentedly, kneading his front feet on his daddy's lap just like a little kitten, Tom settles down to sleep, dreaming not of the sweet taste of mother's milk but of the rather more interesting taste of her blood.

The End

October – Gothic

The Letter

By Anita Ponton

My beloved,

I have wanted to write to you for so long. But they took everything after you left. So, I speak these words; hold them in my head until such time as you can hear them. At night, I repeat them over and over, in the hope that you will hear me in your dreams.

I want you to know that what happened can be forgiven, will be forgiven, when I see you again, when you come back to me.

So I wait and I watch because I know you will return one day. You have to. I still have the key. It's been here with me, all the time. But you will have realised that by now.

I know you are still out there, somewhere, because I can feel you thinking about me, thinking about it, remembering. Knowing this nourishes me, it keeps me here, waiting.

And I know you will come. One day soon.

Waiting here, watching day after day, you feel like you're dissolving into the landscape, eroding, evaporating, turning to dust. Particles upon particles are heaped into endless dunes, stretching out as far as the eye can see. It's like everything and everyone who ever was ends up here, reduced to single grains of eternally shifting sands.

But some things remain, things that can't be eroded by the wind. Things held by memory, thickened by guilt. Echoes. Emotion. Events.

The wind takes everything else.

The old place has changed. I watched as they came to take it all away. I couldn't do anything else, then. I was confused. You had not been gone long. First they took the bed, then the tables, chairs, our clothes, the cups, all of our things. They took it all, loaded it up and drove away. Then there was nothing, except for me. That night, the biggest dust storm I ever saw rose up and blew all the windows out. It was quite something as it roared round and round, shattering the glass, one pane at a time. Suddenly it stopped, almost as soon as it started.

Then the desert claimed the house.

All the same, you were wrong about this place. Nothing really changes. Day after day – how long has it been now? Long enough for the roof to cave in and the door to rust from its hinges. But nothing changes – it just goes on. The sun rises and falls, the wind blows and it never rains. In this arid and rocky land, dry as a bone, hot as Hell, only the wiry scrub endures. No crops grow; there are no seasons, no shadows. No life, just endless decay.

Is that why you brought me here, my darling?

And I watch and I wait.

I climb up sometimes, onto the ledge, to get a better view. Sometimes a car will come, pausing as it passes the house, then speeding off into the hills, leaving only dust slowly settling. Sometimes, although rarely, one will stop. Out they will get, kids - teenagers mostly – curious, apprehensive and bold. Drawn here by rumours and dark whispers, they dare themselves to enter. Wide eyed, they come straight in, without even knocking.

As you know I do not like visitors.

I have learned some tricks while I've been waiting, little things to keep me amused in your absence. I can raise the wind and, if I put my mind to it, I can have it whip up such a storm that it screams like a woman being murdered. Unseen but not unheard, I put on a special show for my unwanted guests, ensuring they leave fast and never return.

One day it will be your car, my darling.

I sleep. Sometimes. When I awake, it seems like years have passed. But always my dreams are of you, of you returning to me, of you joining me here, for good, forever.

You will come soon – I can feel it. I expect the money's run out by now and your dreams will be getting darker. You won't be able to resist.

Even on a still day, hot winds score the surfaces of this barren place. If they should meet, they rise up in angry gusts and furious eddies, becoming briefly the Djin of the sands. Dust devils, biting and rasping, dancing on sand, tearing up everything in their wake. They keep me company.

You told me once that everything in this place vanishes without trace, that absolutely everything disappears forever. And then you laughed. But that's not strictly accurate, is it my darling?

The essence of a thing simply shape shifts, becomes something else. One energy transmutes into another form. It doesn't just go away, it lingers in another guise.

I often think of our last evening together, up in the Star Tower, waiting for the first night stars to rise. How you put your arms around me, to embrace me. Or so I thought. Were you trying to make it look like an accident when you threw me? I don't suppose you expected me to survive that, but when I did you took me down anyway. And now it didn't look like an accident at all. You panicked, my darling. You buried me too soon.

You thought I was gone, but somehow I remain and now I climb the Star Tower every day, to watch for you.

I am the eye of your storm; I am your core, the still point around which everything turns, to which you must return.

I do not fool myself. I know you will not come back for the sake of love or remorse. When you come, I know it will be for the key, the one I hid next to my skin, the last place you thought to look. But you will not get as far as using it.

When you open my grave to dig among my bones, that is when I will take you.

And my forgiveness will be in the form of revenge and I will take you and keep you here with me and I will hold you to me and never let you go and we will be here together forever. Come to me my darling. Come.

The End

November – Steam

The Difference between Mist and Steam

By Peter Collins

Danny Brown peered into the darkness. He was cold and starting to feel uneasy. A mist had descended and lay damp and heavy around him. To Danny's eyes, it seemed to be rising from the ground like steam. He had a brief recollection of the old steam kettle in his grandmother's kitchen. To Danny, steam meant being warm and home and safe. But he was stuck out here in the mist. Mist was cold and damp and horrible. Danny tried to remember the lecture where they had been taught the difference between the two, but his mind was a blank. He simply thought of it as - Steam Good; Mist Bad. He shivered in the dark and cursed to himself.

Two hours earlier, it had been a very different scene. Danny and the rest of the university first XV had been drinking a few pints in the local pub after winning their cup match over a village team deep in the Dales. Word had spread that a convict was on the loose from a nearby facility for the criminally insane, and the boys had volunteered their services to help the police search the area. Buoyed on by beer and bravado, Danny had become separated from the group and was now lost and alone in the gloom. Even worse his phone was still in his kitbag on the bus.

He walked uncertainly forward, his feet slipping on the muddy ground when a sound behind him made him turn. A pale figure appeared through the mist, and Danny sensed a terrifying odour of rottenness and decay. Then something hit him hard in the stomach. He gasped as all the air was sucked out of his lungs and he fell to the floor, his knees heavy in the damp ground. He was aware of a shape standing over him, and a large knife appeared in front of his face. At that moment, someone shouted his name in the distance. Danny was so disorientated he couldn't tell where the shout came from. But the sound had an effect on his assailant. The knife disappeared and Danny saw a shape run away into the night.

His name was shouted again, but Danny was too winded to reply. Painfully, he hauled himself to his feet and stumbled through the mud to the edge of the field. The shout came again, but much fainter this time. By the time Danny had recovered his breath to reply, the searcher had moved away and he was alone again in the night.

Danny lumbered on, his fashionable white trainers slipping and stumbling at every step until he was covered in mud and exhausted from his constant falls. The mist was thick, but the moon was full, and streaks of moonlight cast eerie shadows all around him. At one point he thought he heard a man scream, but he convinced himself it must have been an owl or a fox and he carried on.

After about twenty minutes he saw a light in the darkness. As he neared it, he saw it was an old farmhouse. There was a dented Land Rover parked by a telegraph pole at the side of the house and Danny could see a light coming from the kitchen door beyond. He banged loudly and shouted for someone to open the door. After a moment, the door opened a few inches.

'Who's that?' said a querulous voice.

'I need help,' said Danny. 'I've been hurt.'

There was a pause whilst the door shut, then the sound of a chain being removed. Finally, the door opened and Danny stepped inside. He was in an old fashioned farmhouse kitchen, with a well-worn pine table, a range and a few pots and pans. There was a door leading to the rest of the house and a second door leading to a pantry of some sort. The place was warm, and smelled of gravy. A plume of steam was bubbling from an old kettle on the stove and condensation covered the windows. It triggered memories of his grandmother's kitchen, and all at once Danny felt safe.

He looked at the small old man in front of him. He was a casting director's ideal of a typical Dales farmer. He had grey hair and a pleasant, lined face. He was wearing plain blue work clothes slightly stained with mud. There was a numbered logo of some sort on the right breast obscured by dirt. The old man took in Danny's dirty clothes and his state of unease. He reached for the kettle and made a pot of tea. He poured the tea into two large chipped mugs and then reached for a bottle of whisky from the dresser. He added whisky to both drinks and pushed one across to Danny.

'You take your time, lad,' said the old man. 'Start at the beginning and tell me what's happened.'

Danny began to talk. He told about helping the police, getting detached from his teammates, being hit and ending up here. He felt better after he had talked and the tea and whisky helped.

'If I can just borrow your phone,' he said, 'then I can let my teammates know where I am and I'll be out of your way.'

He was relaxed now, and he smiled the winning smile that he knew worked so well on the parents of the girls he dated. But the old man just shook his head.

'I don't have a phone, I'm afraid,' he said gently. 'They won't put a land line out here; it's too expensive. And my mobile is out of charge.' He pointed at the kitchen window. 'The track down there will take you to the village. It's about four mile.'

Danny began to say something, but the old man anticipated him and cut him off with a wave.

'I'm sorry but I can't give you a lift. I don't like taking my tractor out in the dark. You'll have to walk.'

Danny didn't want to go out in the dark on his own. He wondered what the man would say if he asked to stay there. The whisky and the warm steamy atmosphere had lulled his mind into a bit of a daze.

'I'll go in a minute,' he said. He lifted his cup. 'Perhaps another cup of tea first?'

The old man put the battered kettle back on the stove. As he did so, there was a noise from behind the pantry door. It was only slight, but both men heard it. They looked at each other and Danny saw the old man's eyes nervously flicker to the source of the sound.

Emboldened by the whisky Danny rose to his feet and beckoned the old man to stand behind him. Danny selected a heavy pan from the draining board and held it high above his head. The old man nervously picked up a large knife. Danny reached for the door and pulled. There was a pause and then something toppled into the room. It was the body of a man, perhaps seventy years old. Small and stick thin, with wisps of grey hair. His throat had been cut and the clothing was saturated in blood. His face was stretched in a mask of terror.

There was piercing whistle as the kettle started boiling. Danny turned to see great billows of steam filling the room. Through the haze he could see the old man's leering face and for a moment he could smell the same foul stench of death and decay he had sensed in the field. He felt a knife at his neck, and a flurry of thoughts came rushing through his head as if his mind had suddenly started working again. Why would the old man talk about going out in a tractor when there was a Land Rover by the door? There must be a phone line as Danny had seen the telegraph pole. It wasn't a logo on the blue denim shirt, it was a prison number. Danny knew then that the farmer who had lived here was dead on the floor, and the old man by his side was a deranged killer.

Danny was pushed to a chair and his hands tied to its arms. The old man moved in front of him still shrouded in a curtain of steam. He seemed younger, more rejuvenated, somehow. Danny felt all hope drain from him. He knew he was going to die. A beam of moonlight broke through the window and lit up the old man's mad staring eyes.

Mercifully, some part of Danny's brain had shut down, so he hardly felt any pain as the old man slit his throat. His last thought was of the soft red mist that settled on his arms and face. It was warm and comforting and as he drifted off to sleep he thought that maybe mist wasn't that bad after all.

The End

December – Fire and Ice

Tomar the Terrork Tamer

By Giovanni Cirillo

Many did not wake from their sleep that night and those who did wish they hadn't.

The two Terrorks descended on the small town of Hank in the stillness that was the night. The first Terrork passed over the town unnoticed and unleashed its deadly breath on its sleeping prey. With its mighty wings it lifted itself high into the air joining its partner to get a bird's eye view of what would happen next.

The sleepy guardsman perched on top of his night post leaned forward in his chair. Staring over his peaceful town he felt a warmth rising up inside of him. The warmth quickly turned into a fire and his skin turned cold as ice. He gasped as he felt his inners burning. With the last of his strength he struggled to his feet and reached for the alarm that would warn his fellow citizens of the imminent danger. One pull of the bell's rope was all he could manage before the fire consumed his organs and the ice on his skin froze him where he stood.

∗

- Two years earlier -
Somewhere in the town of Hank.

'Hush, Tomar. Do not let the elders hear your words. You do not understand what they will do to you.'

The boy could hear the fear in his mother's voice as she pulled him into the safety of an abandoned alleyway and hugged him as tightly as she dared. Her tears falling on the back of Tomar's neck evaporated instantaneously. She held on a bit longer refusing to accept the truth.

'Mama, you will burn.'

Tomar freed himself from his mother's arms and watched as the clothes on her body began to smoulder.

'I'm fine my son. They're just clothes. Come we must take you home.'

'No, mama. I'm tired of hiding. I must warn the elders. The monsters are going to come.'

The boy rushed at his mother and gave her a kiss on the forehead then darted into the crowded street. Falling to her knees Tomar's mother wept.

*

- Present day -

A single clang from the warning bell the elders had ordered to be erected two years ago rang through the peaceful town of Hank. Many dead lay frozen in their beds burning on the inside. Those that woke, woke to a distant memory of a crazy boy's ranting about flying beasts.

Bulbar stared through the steel bars between himself and the boy as the noise from the bell rang in his ears. Tomar sat motionless.

'The elders' bell. It… It rang? What does this mean?'

Tomar stood up. His skin glowing from the heat it was generating.

'What does this mean you ask?'

The air turned white as his cold breath left his mouth.

'That bell means the end for the people of Hank. If you do not free me from this prison there is no one that can stop the Terrorks. Please Bulbar. Please be the first person to believe me, to trust me. I've told you all my dreams. Have they not all come to pass? Let me help the people.'

Before Bulbar could respond a great gust of wind shattered the glass of the prison windows and filled the room where the two of them stood. Immediately Tomar felt the coldness inside of him fighting the rising flame as the heat of his skin hissed from the ice trying to form on it. He quickly glanced towards Bulber who was clutching at his chest.

'This is the fire and ice from your dreams Tomar. I'm dying.'

'Open this gate! I can save you Bulbar!'

As Bulbar fumbled to open the gate Tomar closed his eyes and focused on his breathing. He lowered his inner body temperature that the flame inside of him could not burn. Simultaneously he raised the temperature of his skin sending small flames into the air preventing the ice from freezing him where he stood.

The prison gate swung open. Tomar caught Bulbar as he plummeted to the floor. He gathered a breath of cold air in his lungs and as he hugged his captor as tight as he could he released his breath over the dying man. The coldness of his breath restored the man's body temperature while the heat from his skin melted the ice on Bulbar. Tomar gently lowered the unconscious man on the floor and for the first time in two years stepped outside the prison walls.

By the time Tomar reached the streets the two Terrorks had made several passes over the town with their deadly breath. Frozen bodies glittering in the dim light of the crescent moon littered the streets of Hank. Their cold icy-shells holding the burning flames within.

Tears streamed down Tomar's cheeks as he ran with all the speed he could muster. He felt terrible grief for the people of Hank but now there was only one person on his mind.

'Mother!'

He ran through the open front door of the house he once lived in praying that his mother still lived.

'Hello Tomar.'

The three elders who had ordered the young boy to be imprisoned now stood over his mother bound in rope.

'Why are you doing this?'

Tomar's body temperature dropped lower than it had ever been. The air crystallized as he spoke while the flames on his skin whipped at the ceiling of his mother's house.

'Listen Tomar. We always believed you. That is why we had the bell made for this very day. We will release your mother but you need to stop these creatures before it's too late!'

'It is too late. All you wanted from me was your tests. Wanting to know what I was capable of! Well this will be your last glimpse of me.'

Tomar inhaled as much breath as he could find then released it with deadly precision at the men who now held his mother captive. The air crystallized into three ice darts as it travelled towards the elders. Each dart found its mark. Tomar reached his mother as the elders' lifeless bodies collapsed to the floor. Quickly he untied his mother's arms.

'Mama. You need to leave Hank now. Leave through the southern gate. The Terrorks have already laid waste to that part of town. They will only return for their prey once all the people have been killed.'

He helped his mother to her feet. She felt the warmth of her son's skin penetrating hers leaving a faint glow. Tomar breathed gently over his mother's face lowering her body temperature just enough to evade an attack from the Terrorks should they happen to find her. He smiled as he gave his mother a kiss on the forehead then ran outside to meet his fate.

Hank was once again silent. As if the Terrorks had never come and the people were all peacefully sleeping in their beds. The burning crystallized bodies no longer littered the streets. There was no more screaming for help. Tomar wished it to be over as a gush of wind passed over him from the right. Then another from the left. He fell to the floor as a battle of fire and ice waged war both inside his body and on his skin.

'What do I do? What do I do?'

Tomar ripped out the cobblestones in the street as the heat and cold surged through his body. He felt he would soon lose consciousness if he could not regain control. He fell flat on his back in an attempt to relax. As he lay staring up into the night sky he saw the two Terrorks circling high above waiting for him to become a burning fire cocooned in ice. Seeing them slowly descending on him gave him the calm he was looking for. Tomar focused on the heat his skin was generating and pulled it inside his body as he forced the cold in his body to his skin. The fire and ice of his own body met the fire and ice from the Terrork's breath and the particles bonded. Tomar closed his eyes as his skin turned to ice and his body burned.

The two Terrorks came down on Tomar's motionless body. They landed next to him hesitating. The two winged beasts crept closer with their jaws open and teeth showing. Then one leaped forward and swallowed him whole. Screaming they took off into the sky.

Tomar opened his eyes and reclaimed his body pushing the fire inside to his skin melting the ice crystal cocoon and absorbing it into his body. The flames and heat burned the Terrork from the inside out. The creature turned in the air and hurtled towards the ground landing in a curled up heap. Tomar burned his way out of the beast's belly as the second Terrork escaped into the night.

'What does this mean?'

Bulbar stood behind Tomar.

'Please look after my mother Bulbar. I need to tame some Terrorks.'

The End

Bonus Story

The Red Knickers

By Sandra Rose

Francis shook a liberal amount of salt into the palm of his hand and added just a pinch to the pan of boiling water. The rest he discarded over his shoulder, without really knowing the reason why. Was it for luck? He presumed he had inherited one of his mother's many quirks he had witnessed throughout his childhood. Like the way she would pop three painkillers into her mouth before every meal, despite various scans, x-rays, and her Doctor's insistence that there was nothing wrong with her.

He stood in the spotless tiled kitchen surrounded by the cherry wood cupboards that were installed to her specific instructions a year before she passed on. He was staring blindly out of the kitchen window, when he heard Chantelle's beat up Vauxhall pull into the drive, followed by her annoying voice, as soft as a limp handshake, but with the intonation that is pure Essex-girl, rising but never falling like a broken see-saw. He didn't know how Mike could put up with the incessant drivel that came out of that girl's mouth. Not for the first time Francis cursed the day she moved into his home.

Francis had to rent out his mother's bedroom after she died, to help pay the bills. It was a sad time, packing her things into empty lavender scented suitcases and storing them in the loft. Mike had been the first to respond to the advert Francis placed in the Loot. Francis has warmed instantly to the clean-shaven, well-dressed Mike with a boyish sense of humour. The two men lived quite happily together for almost a year. Often Francis would cook a meal which they shared along with a bottle of wine, with stimulating conversations about politics and war, or art and architecture. Other times they would watch a film together in the comfortable silence born from two men who were too tired to talk, but could still enjoy each other's company. But then Mike had met Chantelle, a fitness instructor at the local gym with a tan that came out of a bottle and a pair of tits just as genuine. Two months later Mike had told Francis that she was being evicted and needed somewhere to live.

'You don't mind do ya buddy?' he'd asked, and through clenched teeth Francis had agreed she could move her things in until she found somewhere else. A month turned into two, then it became four, and soon Francis noticed that Chantelle wasn't circling adverts in the paper with her glittery pink pen anymore.

The key turned in the front-door, Francis heard the soft thud of shoes being dropped on the hallway and her voice, louder now, as she took off her coat and bitched about some woman she had encountered at the supermarket. Whenever Chantelle paused for breath he could hear Mike making appropriate noises, trying to sound interested in what she was saying until she ran out of steam. Tonight was the same as every other Tuesday night since she had moved in. Mike went straight to the living room and lounged on the sofa, television remote in hand, flicking between channels in a listless manner. Meanwhile Chantelle unpacked their shopping. As per usual, Francis tried to ignore her presence, which was always hard work. The fridge-freezer resided next to the alcove opening between the living room and the kitchen, putting her in close proximity. Her cheap musky perfume would gradually fill up the room, like a gas chamber, Francis often thought, as he'd feel his throat spasm at the choking effect of her scent. As she placed items in the fridge, she kept up a one-sided conversation with the back of Mike's head.

'I can't believe she had the cheek to say that to me' she twittered on, 'just because she has two kids in a buggy doesn't give her the right...' Francis tried to block her out by focusing on the red and green peppers he now halved a deseeded. Looking over his left shoulder to the beige living room, he could see that Mike continued to channel-hop. Every now and then the volume would go up a few notches, in what Francis suspected was an attempt to drown out her dreadful voice.

After she had finished putting the shopping away, Chantelle headed off to their room. It was her usual night to change the bed, and put the dirty sheets in the laundry. Francis knew this because he'd observed her routine with some disdain. He chopped mushrooms into thin slices, glad for the reprieve from her stifling scent, now replaced by the earthy aroma of the mushrooms. He imagined his mother tut-tutting at Chantelle's substandard housekeeping. His mother had changed the sheets daily, but then his mother was renowned for the pride she took in her house. He placed the sliced mushrooms in a pan of hot oil; and was giving them a stir when over the noise of the sizzling pan he heard Chantelle stomp across the floor.

'What the fuck is this?' she shouted. Francis winced; his mother had hated women that swore. He walked over to the fridge, even though he needed nothing from it, and pretended to examine the use-by date on a carton of milk. He glanced up just in time to see Chantelle standing between Mike and the television; a pair of red lace knickers hung from her right pointed index finger. She was slightly hunched, so she could look down at Mike, her left hand was placed on jutting hip.

Francis smiled as he walked back to the oven. He heard the remote fall to the floor and the batteries roll across the floorboards. Mike's voice was quiet, Francis could just about make out the words 'nothing to do with me' and 'aren't they yours?' above the sizzling pan.

That just fuelled Chantelle's rage as she began yelling.

'Have you ever known me to wear something that looks like it belongs in a brothel?'

Mike's muttered response was too quiet for Francis to make out, but he presumed it was something along the lines of 'if only' because Chantelle was screaming now, and when Francis peeked over his shoulder he saw her face was turning red.

'Oh really? I suppose this would be the kind of thing your into seeing how you're screwing that tart of a research assistant. That's surprised you hasn't it? You didn't think I knew, but I've been onto you for a few weeks now Mike, all those late nights at work.'

'What? I haven't, honestly babe you've got to believe me... I haven't touched Libby, I don't know anything about the...'

'Save it Mike, you're a crap liar.' She sobbed, 'I suppose these are hers' it was more of a statement than a question, Francis peeked over his shoulder again and saw that Mike was peeling the knickers off his head, where Chantelle had just thrown them at him. She turned on her heels and walked resolutely towards their bedroom, as she opened the door she paused and looked back, 'I really can't believe you had the cheek to accuse me of cheating last month over those stupid prank text messages, when all the while...' She paused taking a breath that sounded broken with tears 'When all the while it was you'. She slammed the bedroom door, and then the only sound was the oil spitting in the pan.

85

Minutes passed, Chantelle's crying could be heard through the door. Francis continued to stir the mushrooms, adding the peppers and he poured in some tomato sauce from a jar. The sizzling stopped and was replaced by a quieter bubbling noise. He began to lay the table, taking two placemats out of the drawer, followed by two plates from the cupboard. Two knives and forks followed, a pair placed carefully on the left side of each place mat. He moved a plate slightly; making sure it was centred on the mat. Then he took down some clean glasses from the shelf and placed one almost ceremoniously at one of the place settings. In the other he poured some red wine. Picking up the glass he walked toward the living room and leaned back against one side of the alcove doorway. He saw Mike stood outside their bedroom door, knocking lightly.

'Come on babe, let me in' he whined. Eventually, the door opened, and a more composed Chantelle appeared pulling a small pink suitcase behind her. Her nose was red and her eyes were puffy from crying. Mike grabbed her arm and petitioned her again.

'Babe, please, where are you going?'

She pulled her arm out of his loose grip and sighed.

'Where I go is no longer your concern, I'll collect the rest of my things in the week' she walked past Mike towards the hallway. Mike didn't follow; he just let his arm drop down to his side and watched her leave. She paused, just for one moment, and said sadly 'Of all the places, you had to have her in our bed' before she continued down the hall and out the front-door. Francis involuntarily squeezed the stem of his wine glass. 'Mother's bed' he mentally corrected her. But then he relaxed and smiled, Chantelle was gone! It was just the two of them again.

As Mike turned to face him, he adjusted his face into an expression of friendly compassion.

'I expect you could do with some dinner', he indicated the table with a slight, awkward movement of his hand. 'I've made enough, I mean – it could stretch to two if you want some?' Mike nodded; he had a dazed expression on his face as he approached the table and sat down.

Francis picked up his now half-full glass of wine, whirled around the ruby liquid, and then he drank deeply, tipping his head back and draining the contents. He reached for the bottle to fill Mike's glass and poured himself a rare second glass. Well it was time to celebrate. Perhaps it was too early to tell for sure, but he thought he could see some relief begin to show in the angle of Mike's shoulders, they no longer seemed slumped. They ate in relative silence, a rare blessing since Chantelle had moved in, and so Francis wasn't too concerned about the lack of pleasant banter. He presumed the rakish flat-mate would return with zeal once he had fully comprehended that he was free from Chantelle's smothering grasp.

After the meal, Mike went to his room and shut the door. Francis cleared the table and took out the rubbish. Outside night had drawn in hours ago, and with it frost had begun to settle on the cars parked in the street. Chantelle's Vauxhall was nowhere to be seen, the driveway was empty as

Francis walked toward the pavement. He stuffed the rubbish into the wheelie bin, and then headed back indoors.

He was going to continue tidying up, but Mike was standing in the living room, his hands behind his back. There was an uptight look in his eyes that Francis hadn't seen before.

'Hey Mike, erm... you OK mate?' he asked as he leaned over the sofa to straighten the cushions.

'Oh I'm fine thanks buddy,' Mike replied, approaching the sofa. The edgy look still in place, he continued 'I was just wondering why this was on top of the fridge?' Mike's hands were no longer hiding behind him; they were holding a carrier bag. It was a carrier bag that Francis recognized; it had Madmoiselle Lingerie Shop printed on it. Several tense seconds passed, Francis picked at a loose thread on one of the cushion covers. When he looked up Mike was smiling.

'After the close call with those prank texts, I thought you'd have got rid of this.' With that Mike let the bag drop to the floor as he reached for the remote and slumped on the sofa 'you know what buddy, you're a diamond' he continued. 'I thought she was never going to leave... Dinner was lovely by the way'.

Francis smiled to himself as he headed into the kitchen to retrieve the bottle of wine.

The End

About the Authors

Andrew Newall – The Delivery

January 2015

Theme: Revenge

Nationality: Scottish

Andrew's short fiction has been placed in various competitions over the past few years, including 1st place in the Dark Tales contest in 2010 with *Four in the Morning*, and 3rd place in the Writer's Village short story competition 2012 with a children's story *The Spider and the Bumblebee*. In 2015, in addition to the Writer's Notebook win, his Flash Fiction piece *Wired for Action* was published online in Short Story Sunday. Some of his work can be found online on Short Story Sunday, The Story Shack Magazine, Postcard Shorts and Black Petals.

Read more:

> Flash fiction "The Flight" a flash fiction story is published in "Writing on Water", a 2011 anthology of Flash Fiction and Poetry by Earlyworks Press.

> His short story "Four in the Morning" has been published in the newly-released Dark Tales Volume 16, a collection of horror and speculative fiction stories.

Misty Mikes – My Lady

February 2015

Theme: Bad Romance

Nationality: American

My debut novel *Black Magic* is due to be published in 2016. I studied opera in college, but ended up with a concentration in piano. I spent two years living in an RV and travelling across the country living wherever I felt like at the time, before settling in Lubbock to focus on writing and to give my brother a place to live while he finished his undergraduate. My brother is a math major who works with a super computer that was built to create a realistic zombie apocalypse simulation.

You can find out more information about my book on my blog www.mistymikes.com or follow me on Facebook at https://www.facebook.com/Author.MistyMikes/

Brian Cofflin – Blush

May 2015

Theme: Obsession

Nationality: Irish

 Brian has had a short story published in the *Big Issue* magazine, and another published in *Bunbury* magazine (with include themes such as chance, destiny, circumspection, regret).
He enjoys football, beer, thrillers (books and film) and good company, and is currently looking for a literary agent.

SM Cadman – Foretoken

June 2015

Theme: In the Blink of an Eye

Nationality: Canadian

SM CADMAN is a self-taught fiction writer from some godforsaken city that behaves more like a hick town in Ontario, Canada. She's currently working on a Sci-Fi/Tech/Thriller novel and has a few stories published already. She also has a few more stories and poetry coming out in October and January/February of 2016.

She can be found online at:

http://lunaelektra.com/

https://barriewritersclub.wordpress.com/

On Twitter: @SMCADMAN https://twitter.com/smcadman

Meghashri Dalvi – The Space Child

July 2015

Theme: Isolation

Nationality: Indian

Meghashri has 15+ stories published in English, and 80+ stories in Marathi, a regional language of India.

When not writing sci-fi stories, Meghashri consults in Technical Communication and teaches Management. She is part of the online forum of Marathi sci-fi writers and enjoys participating in science forums, too.

Read more:

http://www.aphelion-webzine.com/shorts/2007/10/TheMountain.html

http://anotherealm.com/2002/flash/blackandwhite.html

Vaun Murphrey – The Bagman

August 2015

Theme: Dystopia

Nationality: American of Irish, English, Bohemian and Native American descent

Vaun Murphrey lives in Lubbock, Texas with her husband, two sons and a shaggy black and white four-legged friend. Her life is composed of one ordinary day after another, at least from the outside – on the inside she travels to different worlds. If Vaun ever seems distracted, now you know why… be patient, she returns on a regular basis to visit Earth.

Read more:

CHIMERA, Weaver Series Book One
CHANGELING, Weaver Series Book Two
VECTOR, Weaver Series Book Three
PHOENIX, Weaver Series Book Four

www.VaunMurphrey.com

www.Facebook.com/VaunMurphreyAuthorPage

https://twitter.com/vaunery

Nicola A. Ferguson – Tom, Tom the Baker's Son

September 2015

Theme: Illusion

Nationality: Scottish

Nicola Ferguson has been many things in her long and varied life: Athlete, Lawyer, Veterinarian (almost), Stunt Woman, Rap God (ha!) and Author. She has recently started writing fiction which she absolutely loves, and one day she intends to return to university in Budapest, and complete her veterinary degree. For the moment, she proudly carries the job description of 'crazy cat lady'.

She came second in another competition with the story 'Black & Grey'. It can be seen at
http://thecultofme.blogspot.co.uk/2015/12/december-short-fiction-contest-winners.html

Read more:

http://nicola-ferguson.weebly.com/

Anita Ponton – The Letter

October 2015

Theme: Gothic

Nationality: British

Londoner Anita Ponton is a multi disciplinary artist and writer of dark fictions. She was educated at Central St. Martins School of Art and at Goldsmiths College. Her art practice is all about the relationship of the body in performance to technology to visibility, representation and space. In her writing she embraces all things Gothic. She has previously had a short story published in a college magazine

Read more:

www.anitaponton.com

www.youtube.com/user/anitaponton

Peter Collins – The Difference between Mist and Steam

November 2015

Theme: Steam

Peter is married with two children and lives in Yorkshire. In his career in marketing communications, he has written or edited hundreds of brochures, leaflets, annual reports and other publications, for web and for print. His freelance business writing has featured in a range of publications included *'Marketing Week'* and *'Direct Response'*. Peter recently gave up full time employment to concentrate on his writing. In that time, he has won a number of short story competitions. His story, *'The Boy Scout'*, is due for publication in early 2016 in *'Voices in the Dark'*, an anthology of short stories published by Bookers Corner. He is currently looking for a publisher for his whodunit novel, *'Captain Goodheart Investigates'*, and for his children's novel, *'The Dagger of Asgard'*, the first of a trilogy.

Sandra Rose – The Red Knickers

Bonus story

Sandra was born in London, and still lives within walking distance of the road she grew up on. She loves to travel, but her main passions are her son, trying to get through her list of '100 books to read before your 40', and writing.

She had her dream job for over ten years, working in a busy bookshop on London's Charing Cross Rd: Shipley Booksellers, an art specialist bookshop and the inspiration for JK Rowling's Flourish and Blott's. When the shop closed due to rising rents she had a change of career, and begun bookkeeping for a highly respected, leading fabric retailer in the heart of Soho.

Following the birth of her son in 2011, she temporarily gave up work to concentrate on her degree, and being a full-time mother.

She graduated from the Open University with a BA Hons Degree in English Literature in 2014.

She currently works as the bookkeeper for an exciting recruitment agency, as well as working on her debut novel and has independently published a small collection of short stories: *The Velvet Cigar* available on Amazon.
ISBN: 978-1493570218

About the Illustrator

Diana Bedrossian

As our contest and anthology is helping to promote upcoming authors, it seemed only right to enlist the assistance of an emerging artist to design the cover. I am delighted with the illustration by Diana Bedrossian which depicts parts of the human brain and heart entwined with an abstract form of anxiety.

As an ethnic Armenian who was raised in Kuwait before coming to the UK to complete an art and design Foundation course as well as to start her current course BA (Hons) Graphic Communications at the University for the Creative Arts, she admits that is no surprise that her artworks and designs are based on conceptual narratives highlighting the topics of identity.

https://www.behance.net/dianabedrossian

Printed in Great Britain
by Amazon